COLORS OF ME

PRACHI BHARDWAJ

Contents

Contents

Contents

Contents

Contents

Embrace every shade of you
From orange to blue

Acknowledgements

I am deeply grateful to so many incredible individuals who have shaped my journey. First and foremost, my heartfelt thanks go to my parents. My mother, Meenakshi Bhardwaj, taught me the invaluable lesson of not succumbing to generational trauma, and my father, Col. Sandeep Bhardwaj, instilled in me the importance of nourishing our roots to thrive and flourish. To my elder sister, Vatsala, thank you for showing me that crying could be therapeutic and for your not-so-weird dance sessions. To my twin, Pranjal, your lessons in self-defense (both literal and metaphorical) have been indispensable and for being there to entertain me, while we were growing up.

I am profoundly thankful to my mentors. Preeti Singh, for teaching me the power of independence and Aneeta Sharma, fellow author and English teacher, for believing in a budding writer.

My heartfelt thanks to my Publishing Manager, Aarthy, for her patience, dedication, and unwavering support throughout this journey. To my therapist, Guntass Cour Sandhu, thank you for helping me believe in myself, for laughing at my jokes (even when they were a defense mechanism), and for gently calling me out on them. Your compassion and expertise have been invaluable, and I wouldn't have reached this point without you.

I had a hunch about what I wanted to do with my life but never knew how to begin. To my college professors, Prof. Asmita Kabra and Dr. Budhaditya Das, thank you for teaching me that hope is the only thing we can hold onto if we want to change the world—even if it's just a tiny corner of it.

To my friends who have become family: Shinjini, my anchor, who taught me to embrace every shade of myself; Misha, for your lessons in empathy and kindness; Neha, for reminding me that prioritizing oneself is never selfish; Janhvi, for being my loudest cheerleader.

To all the extraordinary women who have shown me the beauty of being unapologetically oneself: Niharika Suri, Mansi, Natassia, Kirtika, Sonali, Ritika, Jassi, Sheetal, Nabamalika, Mehak, Samridhi, Nishtha and many others who go unnamed here – you have all been my lighthouses.

Special thanks to Apratim and Suraj, whose stories inspired parts of this book. To Naveen, for all the profound spiritual conversations. To Angad, for showing me the other side of the coin and lastly, to my childhood friends Lt. Ishaan (Bunny) and Dr. Anurati, for your enduring support and friendship.

With deepest gratitude,
Prachi Bhardwaj

Author's Note

I would like to take a moment to appreciate you for picking up this book. After a long battle against perfectionism, I finally present to you my perfectly imperfect book. For as long as I can remember, I was running away from so-called "negative emotions" without realizing I was abandoning myself in the process. There has always been a negative connotation around emotions, and it has been associated with overthinking. I am here to tell you that emotions are not to be categorized into good or bad; they are only meant to be felt. Had it not been for this "overthinking", I would not have been able to finish this book.

Orange and blue are opposites on the color chart, denoting a complete circle of life. We tend to dismiss certain parts of ourselves because we feel they are not acceptable to society. Unless we don't embrace and accept our own selves, we will never fully be able to experience any emotion. Be it anger or love. Be it anxiety or trust. We will never be able to see beyond our narrow minds. There's no such thing as true love without first embracing your true self. These colors contain various hues within them, as the poems cover different shades of moments.

There are many things that happen to us which are not in our control. In fact most of the things aren't. Hence I don't blame kids when they have a prejudiced mindset. But as adults it is our responsibility to unlearn. I am proud of you, if you even managed to unlearn one thing that was ingrained in the deepest depths of your brain and if that helped one person. Even if that person was you.

LOVE

Is This Poetry?

Is it supposed to rhyme or be a mismatch

Is what I used to wonder about when I was a youngster

I started to feel poetry before I could write one

Started to feel the pain in my vein and the beauty of it in my brain

Desperate to make sense of the nights that leave me in fright

I pour to make myself feel light, but on most days, I have to fetch the words to not overwrite

Some are the right words in the wrong line, and the rest are wrong words, not helping me rhyme

But is it supposed to rhyme or be a mismatch? I wonder, at times

All This While

I was falling, crashing and crawling
All the while, you stood there watching
I was hurting, crying and begging
All the while, you trembled while staring
I was healing, talking and walking
All the while, you were smiling
I was all better with gleaming eyes that I failed to hide
All the while, you never left my side

Platonic Love

Not every story is a love story
and not every love story is worth the history
Not every chapter of the history is worth the glory
All the lovers in these chapters that have loved before me
Have missed the strongest of love that has radiated toward me
The kind of love not worthy of any mention
That skipped everyone's attention
That exists without any expectations and in all dimensions
Pushing all limitations
This love has been the one I got to choose and has led me to the most
beautiful views

Love is Love

Everyone is telling me whom to love

In old times, people like me are sent to the hell above

Reciting that there's nothing wrong with me each night

In the darkness of injustice, I could see the light

I don't have to redefine myself for you to love yourself

Your cussing and beating will not lead me into conceding

I wish I didn't waste so much time trying to justify the false crime

The old me has not died

This is a discovery that I don't have to force myself to hide

Best Friend

I need you like strings for a guitar
I need you like a bow for a violin
and I'll be lost without you, like a page without a bookmark
You held me at my lowest
and laughed with me at my best
I don't know how, but you see through my unspoken words, my dry tears
and my shaky ground
You comfort me, at times with a nod and at times with a monologue
You be the snake, and I'll be the venom
You be the moon, and I'll be the stars
You be the colors, and I'll be the brush
Without you, I am a song without a melody
You make yourself hate the same people as I
You know, when I want to hear the hard truth
and when I want to stay in my sky
You take me for who I am
You vex me, and you save me at the same time
You are my safety net
You are my harness
You are the piece that completes my mosaic

Hold me Tight

Everything comes with an expiry date
and if we turn into a sad fate
Then, hold me close until the morning light
I want to love you hard and love you right
Unwind every scar and kiss you all night
Unplug the words that are stuck in my head like a rusted phonograph
My faith is as loyal as the words coming out of a stenograph
With you, I want to watch the sky change from afterglow to amber
Ready to bet on us like a gambler
When I'm with you, I hear the wind sigh in disbelief of my lucky luck
These caramel-colored eyes have been my best prize
The crease around your lips
with the wrinkles around your eyes,
is my favorite kind of smile

Self

Body hair and stretchmarks
Uneven skin tones and pockmarks
Firms creating insecurities out of normality
Pushing us all away from the reality
Ashamed of the stitches and scars
These are your own stars
Fine lines and wrinkles bridge the gap between the young and the wise
Make way because there are different forms of love yet to recognize
Tossing and resisting these internal routes
While I see the young lacking the roots
Self-pity won't keep you grounded
Self-compassion and empathy are to be founded
Stop trying to fix something that isn't broken
You can't have holes in your loyalty
Loving your own self is the only royalty

Waltzing Around the World

One day, I decided what I wanted
The things I've been running from
are the same things I was running toward
And so I dashed
And so I crawled
While the house howled
and while the roads roared
Displeased from me
Mortified by all that they
couldn't be
While the girls and boys begged
"Take my worries away too."
While the adults around me yelled
"She has always been the selfish one,
between the two."
And so I dashed
And so I crawled
For I couldn't save anyone at all
Burning all the shackles through
my rage and cape
Saving the only life I could save
And so I dashed
And so I crawled
I was accompanied

by the fallen leaves and the dancing trees
and as the water waved at me
I saw the sun gleaming at me
and the wind whispered
in the sound of an elf
"You only live for one, yourself."

Constellations

I never tried remembering constellations
because then I'd look for them
in the sky rather than myself

Am I Not in Love?

They say I'm to feel stifled if you're not around
When in touch with you, a missing piece of me is found
All the ballads are to remind me of you
And for everything, you are to be my muse
They say your touch is enough to melt my agony
That the taste of your curse would be sweeter than jaggery
But as seasons passed
From being a teenager to an adult at last
For me, love doesn't feel like that anymore
It's as if I'm at peace and, at times, at war
The butterflies seldom come to visit me
Love for me is like watching the sunset on the sea
Where my sky is of numerous hues
And each is necessary to paint the perfect picture
Where every color in my life is important for the mixture
Love for me is not sheltering me under an umbrella
While you drench in the rain
It is for us to share
Love for me is to not project my fears and insecurities onto you
But to see myself as a mural and you as a mirror
Where I could self-reflect each shade of me clearly
Love for me is not you snatching my grocery bag from my hand
But to know the importance of my independence and understand

Love for me is to not find solutions for you
It is to walk with you even when I'm unsure of the view

AGONY

First Failure

The last day of June gave me my first best friend
Eternal affection was bound to end
The tonic of silent hate you drank from your mother's hand ran in her
family
Wrote letters, but now they have no receiver's address
You never wore our matching dress
You wanted to shape us without me
Kept the key close to you, never letting me free
My first love got lost by loving too hard
I battled between keeping hope and letting go
I was in a new low
You changed sides faster than I could flip a coin
Lovelorn in this lonely abode
I forgave you in an instant, telling myself you were a kid
Forgot to remind myself that, and so was I
Why was I not worthy of your love?
It is a mystery from above

I still whisper your name in the darkness of the void while holding our
polaroid
I still feel the outline of my scars, but at least now I don't soothe myself
in bars
A faint smile paired with watery eyes appears while I reminisce about
the time I was unwise

I fell for your tears but never for my bleeding heart
I battled between keeping hope and letting go
This time, I hope I don't fail to let it all go

Is This What You Call a Home?

Surmised as a safe space, but it's a place where I poured my heart out and was beaten
Where my people haunted me more than my own demons

Is this what you call a home?
Where I was made to watch my innocence fade away
Where every day was a doomsday

Is this what you call a home?
Where I got more shame and grief to carry
My coffin will be too heavy to even bury

Is this what you call a home?
Where I was a stranger to my own shadow
Where the grills on the windows felt like a prison ready to swallow
I couldn't share or bawl due to the paper-thin wall

Is this what you call a home?
Where everything was foisted on me, and my decisions were made for me
Blood is thicker than water, but only I held my bleeding heart during the manslaughter

Is this what you call a home?
Where I was reminded of my unfinished drafts before carving a new craft
Where there were only critics around
Where every waking moment, I devised plans to not stay on this ground
Can I even take it anymore, or will this be my evermore?

Give Me Back My Girlhood

Stripping off the shields of a child
so you could leave the memories you had with her behind
Showing true care until I believed what you used to swear
Pulling down my barbed wire
You went ahead and set my skin on fire
Trusting an older guy would be more mature
You accused my intentions despite them being pure
I gave everything I could to you at nineteen
Soon, the devil turned my favorite place into a crime scene
Stopped being candid, couldn't give you what you demanded
Was added to your list of being abandoned
I miss how I used to swing around without paying heed to the ringing
bells
Now, I walk on spiked eggshells
You held my hand, and I flushed
All grew suspicious, and only I was being crushed
You planted a tree for me and then watched it die
You were too ashamed of who you were, so all you did was lie

Unfair Justice

The great anger clouding my judgment

My body reacting on its own as if my mind has gone for a stroll

My senses coming back, I realize what I did

Turned into the people I hate

You vex me. You no longer want texts from me

Want to be invisible; not sure if I won't repeat it this time

but your bitter words were much worse than the crime

Your retribution only created a fusion between my two personalities

*Polarized me for a petty crime when, in reality, people are generally left
with a warning sign*

Telling myself others got it worse

I still catch myself crying in remorse

Told you my worst fears

You went ahead and did those

Fingers and toes crossed for you to realize this was too much of a cost

but your hatred only augmented

and there was no waiver despite my best behavior

For the Highs

Nobody can love me the way you did
Even you couldn't keep up with the love you promised
Loveless and stranded
Euphoria has left me abandoned
How you, as a lover, soaked the seed of misery
It will be a mystery
Only there for the high
Left me alone in my low-to-die
For you, I would have dug graves
But you dashed to the shore the second we were hit by the waves

Nightmare

Oblivious of why I was surprised by a scorpion's bite

These are the stings that bleed in my dreams

and in my dreams, I try to pinch away the pain

and in my dreams, I am screaming voiceless screams

and in my dreams, I am sprinting without moving

and in my dreams, I am falling while standing

and in my dreams, I try to save the dead from the living

How many times will I have to read the same chapter in different books?

I wish I could expectorate the colors of my nightmare

Deceitful

A barking dog that bites
Everything has to be about you
If you are not the center
You feel like an outlander
Surprising how you manipulate others for North
while the compass is in their hands
How you torment people and find it pleasurable
An avid reader yet ignorant of the importance of words
Being deafening doesn't make you heard
Twisted the wires of my brain
I can't remember my own name
Innocent smile with a conceited mind
You walk around with Jekyll and Hide
You cheat and lie, then beg for mercy and blame it on your spite
Always have reasons for why you are right
Making everything seem so white
Thinking others aren't that bright
You are proud of being cunning
I hope you soon have an awakening

The Woman I Became

The world I fight with is my own
The person I keep proving my worth to is in my bone
I purposely find the things to fill my hands with
Even when they are bruised from withy
I am either guilty of the work I haven't started to do
Or overwhelmed with how much I have to
I am the woman who never outgrew
I am the woman who fought hard but never got rescued
I am the woman who talked about it but eventually ran from the view
They chose to be blind
and I to be silent
I melted the bars of these cages with my words
but did not have the nerve to fly away like birds

The Adult Kid

I'm the island you're looking at from the waters
You want me to take care of the people you're meant to love
and when I call you out for not showing up,
all you do is interrupt
Kept all my broken glasses to myself
To be called a "good girl."
To be called the "easy child."
The one who never needed much care and attention

I'm the one who never got to be a child in her childhood
I'm the one who parented her parents
I'm the one who took all the daggers that were
being passed down through generations
I'm the one people labeled "the rebel."
and if I spoke out of my turn, "the sentimental."

Nobody came to my rescue at the gallows
I'm the one who was her own prey, and arrows
I'm the one who traded civility for memories
I'm the one who only had her own shoulders to caress
Learned how to take care of myself
while they justified
"at least we are not swaddling you in your sleep."

The one who became the adult she needed as a kid
The one who strode through the wilderness
while holding her own hands
And the one who would do this all
over again at another chance

While everyone was submitting their research papers
While everyone was falling in love and celebrating their anniversaries
While everyone was shaping their lives with perfect timing
I spent years in surviving
I spent years unhearing the words
that people spoke
I spent years reminding myself
that my words weren't mine anymore
and I spent years re-building the house
that I never broke

Unscripted

Bullied myself for decades to be a perfectionist

The concept of "never giving up" sold to me at a price of my own peace

Podcasts after podcasts

Trying to push me for something that I was meant for in my past life

If I switch too fast, they throw "I told u so" and tag me as "unfocused."

I kept count of the masters whenever my crayons would go out of the line

The depth of frustration got too high

I want to wear my mistakes, like marks on my knees from learning how to walk

My body dissected into a rigid dichotomy

Took me years of tears and sleepless nights pacing

To break the chains, I was embracing

To know I am better off being a jack

I will do everything to fit perfectly, like water

I will pour myself from one vessel to another

No, I am not taking passion for habit

The one who gives up is a " loser", but

the one who tries something to find out

it wasn't made for her happiness has no name

Everyone Be Quiet

I don't want to be told, "It will be okay."
I don't want to be told that it is just another day
I just want to be swaddled into your arms
Even if it's for a second, I just want to feel
the warmth of another body
I don't want to be wise
I just want to be immature
I don't want to be strong
I just want to feel the hurt during this storm
For I can't walk any longer without trembling down
And I can't have a brave spirit when
everything in the universe is incoherent
I don't want you to tell me what to do
I want you to sit with me while I get through
That it is normal to feel what I am feeling
and if I hold on a bit longer, I will have a prettier view

Empty Trysts

Growing together also meant growing apart
I watched the haze appear and disappear
I watched the interlocked hands unlock
Loving someone also meant being vulnerable
I watched the arcade turn into separate rooms
I watched the food go cold
Spending time also meant losing your space
I watched the new fence around our favorite place
I watched you walk away with grace
Playing games also meant losing one
By the end, the only color we wore was blue
By the end, the only thing left to talk about was the view
and by the end, I almost fell in love with you

Rein

A person who failed to notice my screams
Would never dare to hear my whispers

FRACTURED WALLS

Morning Fights

Your unresolved issues dragging everyone on the stand, making us all take sides
It was all bearable until you brought your kids to the war fields
Minding our way through our rooms with broken plates lying everywhere like still and cold pieces of your heart
So self-centered in proving your point you fail to see how much further you are going to disappoint
Crawling under my bed sheets, hoping it'll transport me to a happy place, but all it can give is
the darkness
which somehow always leads me into calmness
Trying my best to stay away from all these drugs
To silence the voices in my head, I turn the volume up of my earplugs
After your mouth running curses, I spend weeks running miles
And in the end, I was in the sun with the light reaching my eyes
and it was only my hand, which was made by both of you, that was stopping the light from passing by

Swinging Egos

Baseless screams, both the voices are at fault

Blinded by their drive

All souls only want to defend their egos

They feel too superior to look inside

Women coming in the middle to avoid strangling the necks

Get pushed aside, hitting their heads

The swinging egos are only looking for faces to blame

Jumping to conclusions only to win these lordly games

The last man standing takes the crown regardless of the age difference

Everyone wants to be indifferent

They go to release their tension in the bar

Aloof of the man-made scars

Putting "men have anger issues" on the stand is like a verdict being passed without looking at the crime

We always have to let go and talk in whispers because it will only worsen the time

Body shivering after watching the fights throughout the day, week, month and year

Bombarding empty ideas to help myself cheer

Now, even the voices inside my head are a reflection of my fears

Trying to find new places to go to find my lamented inner peace

Scouring this town to get all the bad memories released

Infidelity

Now I know what passwords are for

He was using it to hide his hideous crimes

God cursed me for cracking the code, but Satan had already cursed my household

One man's urge pains more than scourge

All my heart was being ripped out, but I had to be strong when my mother was around

Trying his best to erase his second life after chasing younger females out of spite

You give the power of love to someone, and they use it for evil

He wants the queen and the mistress despite the upheaval

We should have seen the mercurial atrocity

I wonder if this crime has taken place frequently, with this being the only time he's been caught

All these stolen moments with clandestine meetings were adding up to many miseries

Can hear the broken tears with this pain being so brutal, making us lose faith in humanity

Didn't know that the protector of the realm could be a part of such calamity

Feels like I can see the air particles

Is this an end or just an obstacle?

Don't know what's right or wrong

Every breathing moment seems prolonged

'Breathe your way through', but how do we breathe when someone takes our lungs away?
Can't remember how my past used to look like
Can barely remember what the touch of a father felt like

Bouquet of Dead Roses

Abridging my words in a tremor because you always had a temper

Fixing all the bad habits you picked up as a kid to explain the actions that you did

We weren't meant to celebrate from the very beginning; I was at the detriment

Wasting my breath to patch up your mistakes

Should have listened to my gut before the outbreak

Counting the aligned stars on the ceiling while bleeding from the shards on the ground

I let you love me in your dysfunctional way, forgetting that I don't have to decay

I chose myself last so you could choose me first

The beatings I bore could never be reimbursed

Wasting my breath to patch up your mistakes

Should have listened to my gut before the outbreak

Not believing my eyes or my mind

Falling for your words and not the times you were unkind

From cursing me to giving me a bouquet of dead roses

More bad than good dozes

Wasting my breath to patch up your mistakes

Should have listened to my gut before the outbreak

Kept screaming your ungrounded principles in reply

I turned a blind eye

Pummeling my soul with your leather belt and your cursed words

at least I will get a bouquet again tonight, is what I was told
Wasting my breath to patch up your mistakes
Should have listened to my gut before the outbreak
The final burst led me out of that house with prolific burns on my crease
This time, I won't recede
This time, I will listen to my gut to save what remains of me

Children of the War

Comrade's blood and the mud is interlaced

People falling asleep in intervals with the ammos chased

I belong to this side of the barbed wire

Which is enough to decide the right and wrong

Blood splashes in my dreams

Visions of violet and maroon spots on people through the ambulance beams

These ghastly scenes are all I see

My peace lies at the end of the sea

Over my head, I hear the vultures squawking

for now, I have become a dead man walking

A daughter, a wife, a sister, and a niece are all frantically pacing

Waiting for their loved ones to return

Shrieking screams come from the ones who are beaten by the men who returned after many shags

Muffled cries for the ones who came swaddled in the flag

Need to keep going, as she has a child to bear

With no nickel to spare

I harbor tremors of watching my clothes ripped

Being silenced is the cause of me being an addict

All I can dream of is being taken away by the enemy

I am a criminal without a felony

Took away my family by blowing up my place

I only dream of my mother's embrace

If I had one wish, I would wish for my brother's life

If I had one wish, I would wish my head on the knife

I will seek vengeance even though all I want to do is beg for mercy

but am I my father's son if I let their death be unworthy?

I want to go back to school; I want to play with my friends

What flashes before my eyes are the pierced bullets in my allies

I was told this was a noble way to die, but I only saw terror in everybody's eyes

Soldier Without a War

The storms never bother me anymore
My dreams are all about the flashbacks now
I am never in my house
The colors of war have engulfed my mouth
Things that slip from my tongue are only war cries
There is no glory in the prize
I am under a spell
Constantly in a place I can't tell
Standing over clean, glistening glass
I miss the howl from the mass
An addictive poison in an eternal prison
Extending my hand, I can still touch the mud
Having breakfast, I can still taste the blood
and the storms don't bother me anymore
'Tis the raindrops, soft and gentle, that I can't ignore

"No Privacy" Prevailed

My secrets were stripped naked

Everyone saw right through the world I had created

They failed in their explanation

and I was forced to give a justification

Mocking my rolling tears

I stood there alone on the stairs

There were no thoughts they had not read

There were no secrets left that they had not spread

People got hurt, people got loved

People succumbed

But not me

I stood there silently

Terrified to take another step

Risking my privacy that never prevailed

Walking naked while they all had their secrets wrapped

I still get shivers around my abusers

but I have got long monologues for the strangers

Intruder

Traitor, traitor, you crossed my body
Outside and inside, you left your mark all around me
Peeling my skin off to erase your touch
It always comes back to me when I least expect it
A flash of a moment sends me back to the place of the tragedy

Your greed left me starving forever
Tracing my skin in all the places giving you pleasure
Leaving me tormented
I let you reside in me, not knowing
what it was that was making you spill all over me

I had a vision
A vision of me yelling
A vision of taking your hand out of me and running
A vision of me finally breathing
And that's all I got
A vision
Because traitor, traitor, you crossed my body
Outside and inside, you left your mark all around me

Numb

I saw a toddler cry bleakly
I wonder what it feels to be able to feel this deeply
Without feeling guilty about bothering others

DESPAIR

The Air Between Us

All the unsaid emotions linger in the air

Adding to the bridge, we didn't know we had to bear

You're hanging by a rope, and I by a thread

I want to rescue you, but I need to be saved first

Tell me the words I can whisper to you,

help me lift this guilt before another outburst

I'm walking toward you among dry woods

Being a matchstick, I try my best to be careful of what I say

because I'm terrified of setting your forest on fire on my way

I know this is the life you think you deserve

Pushing yourself off the curve

I hope the air between us will carry these "too sensitive to be said" words

Self-hate is all that runs through your nerves

We have drifted away like never before

You are not to be seen anywhere from the shore

Will my desperate voice reach you even if I roar?

but you're hanging by a rope, and I by a thread

I want to rescue you, but I need to be saved first

Tell me the words I can whisper to you; help me lift this guilt before
another outburst

Burned Out

Carry me! Someone carry me!

I'm exhausted

Can feel the fatigue running in my veins

Trying to wash away these stains

My body is tired from running a phantom marathon that I just lost

But they expect me to run another at my cost

'Losing' and 'exhausted to win' are different

I want to crawl, but I can't be ignorant

Carry me! Someone carry me!

Or I'll lose everything, and they'll get to say

I never tried anything

"You don't deserve this break."

Persistence and fluidity can co-exist

You don't always have to resist

Tip Toeing in my frantic paces around my room

Searching for some certainty in the uncertainty

My patience is becoming unsteady

I compare myself to others who are happy

and here I am, spending all my energy surviving

With daily internal breakdowns and shivering shoulders

My baggage is getting heavier with each callous comment of yours

Watching myself from the ceiling above

Silently screeching my way out of the abyss

I don't know how long it will take for me to recharge, and I have no
words to reach out

Peer Pressure

Young and old, both are swiping left and right
to fill the other side of their beds every night
I don't want to be a part of this phantom race
but I don't seem to be handling this with grace
The loneliness creeps in at midnight
and I'm feeling less hopeful after each daylight
Don't want to belong to anyone
On some nights, I just want to be held by someone
I don't know how a lover would make a difference
but everyone suggesting sounds confident without any evidence
I seem to be living under vigilance
Asking to lower my standards; every detail shouldn't matter
Shall I be too distant from myself to be close to someone at this age?
Gasping for air in a pool of rage
Have started feeling the pressure
The pressure that is stealing the hope for the future

Watch

The cuts on your wrists are turning into scars
They are fading, but their marks will remind us of the battles you lost
I want to say the right words at the right time
To help your darkness surrender to the light
but I always tend to fall short
Is there anything more I can do than to sit and watch you merely survive?
Is there anything more I can do to help you not hate being alive,
to help you rescue from the night you've been in for an eternity?
If heaven could speak, would they be able to save you from this mundanity?
One can only save those who want to be saved
Watching is all I can do
Watch your skin turn from brown to blue
New scars in the places that are your private spaces
Watch you turn into dust like you were cursed

Sober

I want to take you home

Driving on a road between the loam

The liquor is the only blood running in your veins

Please hold on to what remains

I want to love you, right, despite our fights

You say you are fine, but I know you think of jumping off the cliff when
you drive

You threw away the filled bottles on an impulse

Your pain continues to form ripples

You couldn't outrun the withdrawal

I know you are exhausted from this quarrel

But I'll love you right when you fail to see the light

You're intoxicated, tumbling and dreading

I'm shivering, screaming and begging

Let me fight your demons in all seasons

The liquor is the only blood running in your veins

Please hold on to what remains

You say you are unworthy of love, and the mighty sighs in disbelief from
above

He won't stick around longer, is what I heard from the doctor

Please let me love you right through your violent nights

Estrangement

And my old self would not have believed the existence of this day

All the promises are just meaningless words now

I'd kill for you, but I don't have anything to share with you

We are here, and I already miss you

How did we drift so far apart?

In a world where we promised to be the ocean and the waves;

now, we are no different from the sun and the moon

We've outgrown each other while wearing our gifted sweaters

I hold our memories close to my mouth; they spill every time someone

asks me about good times

There isn't a day that goes by where I don't reminisce about your face

But with you here, the old me goes silent

You can't read my mind like the old ways

And I don't have the strength to tell you about my days

Thank you for all the shrouded memories, even if it was just a phase

Penniless

So many daggers yet to be pulled out
I shift my gravity, and they bleed out loud
People count me as their shield
Yet I am armorless when I plead
Have lost all threads of trust
I am penniless when I buy faith
Don't want anyone to go through this phase
Hence, I take care of each detail
People count me as their shield
Yet I am armorless when I plead

From an Addict

Everybody is on a run

Answering phones for me

In this rehab, we get everything apart from getting free

It's all in my head, is what they told

My soul seems to be sold

Used liquor for my triggers

Nothing matters until I see my loved ones

I want to get better, but my heart only succumbs

The way things are going

I know all this is not working

Popping drugs to get free from alcohol

Being sober is an alien concept after all

It's a fight that's getting old

I don't want to be defined by this anymore

But there's nothing new in this abyss

I'm Not a Lover

I'm not a lover
I'd pull off my skin to cover you
I'd break my bones to make a bridge for you
I'd slice out my heart for you to feel how it bleeds for you
I'd be happy to carry my saviors complex
if that's what love feels like to you
I'm a giver in a greedy herd
I'm the bread in a starving world
And I'll walk away from you once you've unfurled

To My Eating Disorder

You speak to me
when the lows get too low
and when the void gets too loud

You whisper into my ear
Making food my greatest enemy
The world spins for eternity
and I have lost my identity

Pinch some salt on your tongue, and you'll be fine
Press your stomach a bit longer
and you'll make it through the night
Be a bit more slender, and then
he'll call you "mine."

I'd rather faint than eat
I'd rather spit than swallow
You have a false perception
and I've only known deception

I know it will get better
I know I will learn to like food
and I'll push through the days
when I'm not in the mood

You are not an enemy
You are just a false perception
and I am only trying to come back
to this dimension

In My Room

My room is a sponge
Walls have swallowed all the screaming
The pillow has soaked all the tears
Books have heard all my unfinished speeches
Mirror has locked away all my insecurities
The shower released my anxiety down the drain
A wardrobe filled with all my folded personalities
My demons hung up on the hanger
While my body sinks in the bed

Wrath

A black cloud covers my mind

I can see things but can't distinguish

I only see myself being anguished

All the colors become one

When I'm genuinely hurt

I force myself to not blurt

because my thirst for retribution will only make things worse

If they ask who hurt you the most?

My mind always whispers my name

I count to five

The only thing that goes on in my mind is to not strive

Deafening trembling makes me feel heard

Force them to swallow the pill of bitterness I feel within me

created by the words said to me

They commit a crime, and I a sin

Then aren't we from the same kin

I miss you

If you asked me what I'd want to hear from you
It'll be the words
"I miss you", not "I love you."
Because the former holds more truth
And you would've said the same,
had you been fooled like me in your youth

Anxiety Attack

The one who befriended me without my knowledge
Paying me visits during my solace
The cold puff of air filling my blood vessels
The brain fog spreads like a black cloud
Being stifled within a crowd
I could hear the drum beats in my mouth
My skin turned purple as if I was poisoned
Ears shutting off, silencing all the voices around
Is it something that I ate?
Is it an earthquake?
Bombarding myself with questions
Trying to figure out the equations
Until it passes away
Leaving me in fright
What seems to be on the surface
Is not even close to what's underneath
And even though now I know the answers to these questions
I'm still afraid of my friend
Because when it visits me,
Everything seems to come to an end

I only want him

My friends slammed the door
And my lover and I prepared for the war
It was the kind of love everyone knew
would be the end of my sanity
He was the magician, and I became his muse
Using all his new tricks on me to amuse

I had to give up all my loved ones to be able to love you
The way the women in the past sacrificed their identities
For their husbands who only knew the language of lust
The way the women held onto the hope of gleaming light
among the gray skies

I hated them
For they never thought of themselves
I hated the things that love made them do
Forsake themselves to let their beloved in

Now, I have become those women
Who are intoxicated in their own haze
Would do anything to feel his gaze
I have yet again pushed my happiness off the roof
To let you into the room

The magician who made me his muse
Swaying me in half and then asking for a truce
My family slammed the door
Only I prepared for the war

LOATHING

Fire

The fire in me is cursed

Sometimes, the spell gets reversed

Causing a cloudburst

The fire in me was there to guide me

but it only ended up pulling me away from being free

It doesn't distinguish between the good and the evil

I want to be good for you but don't get too close, as this fire will engulf everything you admire

This fire in me was meant to protect me from any burns, but the tables turned

Now I'm protecting your love from getting burned

My ferocious anger won't see if you were the one to cause the hurt

Your affection was to be water, but it only acts as fuel to the flame within me

Don't get too close

It's better to burn myself than another soul

Greed

We are all made of greed

Greedy for more love than we can offer

Greedy for more money than we can work for

Greedy for someone to listen to us without working on our emotional disability

Greedy for blaming others than taking accountability

Greedy for less fat on our body

Greedy for drugs to inject that can't be handled by antibodies

Gulping whiskey then making hospitals a million-dollar industry

Greedy for territory, fighting wars for glory

Oh god, will I ever be satisfied, or will chasing things be how I end my story?

A faded artist

You were the centerpiece
but the eyes were caught only by the masterpiece
The number of people who showed up was four, and now all are bored
You wanted to be a figment of the race, but you didn't fit into this place
You carved your heart out on the canvas the way you were told
but they found someone else's blood rarer
All the sweat ripped like an old pair of jeans from the seam
Your copper hair turned gray by the second it seems
Devoid of passion and rolled up in a barren land, which once was a
lush foliage
Now you've got a rusted mind from the anxiety and the pressure
The beauty that once crawled up in your art is no longer a treasure
You are a faded artist whose art will make it to a few pages in history
The passion that used to be your escape road is now a haunted abode

Scattered Wires

Where are we going

We did all the grinding

The failure pushed me toward substances

I know what I am isn't defined by these instances

The fog in my brain has reappeared

All I see is all I've ever feared

Mumma, hold me tight

I didn't turn out to be so bright

The truth stripping my insecurities and layering it into the reality

I want to push myself from the wall

However, only I'll be there to pick myself up from the fall

There was no light in the room

So I pushed the roof

I can see the sunbeam, but I don't feel the gleam

These scattered wires of my brain are wrapped around my body like an iron chain

Making it hard to breath

I know I want to surrender underneath

Everywhere I reside over and over, once again, the fog rides

Burning me under the skin

The only thing my vision sees is the darkness surrounded by fear

I want to cry, but I am unable to shed a tear

I'm sinking, and I don't know where we are going

Birthday Blues

Can't afford unanswered calls
Glad you all remembered
but all I want is to spiral up in my bed
It might sound selfish
but I don't want to be asked about my plans
I have emptied all the cans
Thank you for all your gifts
I sincerely hope my mood shifts
Showing my teeth forcefully
For y'all to think I have accepted the day gracefully
Counting my stars and then being outweighed by the scars
My favorite thing to do is to be left alone
but I think, for some reason, a party and a blissful time are what I owe
Want to be happy, but only for you all

Wild

Begging me to trust myself again
Standing in a familiar lane
Planted trees all by myself, and now I'm a stray here
Running in a circle
No exit near or far
Forcing myself to not end up at the bar
Part of a phantom race
I learn lessons at a snail's pace
Yet I end up in the same place
Don't give myself the room for mistakes
Don't know when I will stop looking for a face to blame
Retracing the footprints I left when I was strolling through the woods blind
The negative words of the spirits around me and my words of wisdom are all intertwined
All this is happening inside the wilderness of my mind

Reflection

I can be anything I want to be

Then the night comes as a question of my worth

Successfully vanquishing my self-esteem

Is there ever going to be a better me?

My inconsequential past acting as evidence

I can deal with the negativity, but my reflection is what stops me

Crawling out of the mirror and dragging itself with my resilient body,

hoping the baggage would stop me

Ponder how many failed minds are of such kind

The seed of fear of failure was sowed when I failed my first test

Ever since then, it has been a fight to prove myself

The fruit is other's approval

While I sit in silence, burning my pages because I never liked what I

wrote

Other's applause in the morning, and I curse myself at night

On the other side of the illusionary line of chalk lies my perfect self

Will Someone stay?

At times, I can't stop seeing the sparkle in my eyes
but most times, I can't stop running from the dullness of my own soul
I feared being abandoned, but as I grew up, I realized I was terrified
of the people who stay
As their actions make less sense to me than of those who walked away
I feel an ache in my chest on hearing a compliment and am satisfied on
hearing a cynical criticism
I am a wide surface with no depth
Even with bloodshot eyes, I never let someone hold me whenever I wept
I am a good listener, but I'm not the girl who gets chosen at the end
I am the stranger you befriend
I am the lover who leads you to "the one."
She'll get the filtered version you'll become
I am the soul that helps you find yourself
Leading a life of rich experiences filled with gratitude
On the contrary, I build things to tear them apart, to end up in solitude
I am a paradox who loves herself temporarily
People will come and go momentarily
But will someone stay with me in this dismay?
Knowing there resides a silent cyclone within me
In a forest of daisies, would you still pick me

Seasonal Depression

Short mornings and days filled with fog

Festival after festival reminds me of all the people up in the air, along with my dog

Used to look forward to this some ages ago, with family rituals being mandatory

Now the wind is slapping my bare skin as a form of mockery

Want to curl up in bed and be a deadpan

Getting addicted to some kind of sadness like a madman

Abandoning all the faces like my thoughts being locked up in cages

I can see the character disparities with seasons changing

Finding new reasons to be happy to get myself out of this without drowning

Sequester

I am trying to make sense of the blood I bleed
The love I never got to receive
My whole childhood was a lie
Watched all the wandering souls pass by
How was I to believe in love
when all I ever saw were broken, dysfunctional hearts being shoved?
Held onto hope no matter how small
Kept the frames all over the wall
The false memories were much sweeter than the reality
An infant who was liked because of premature civility
Though I disliked being coddled, they called me wise and mature
All I ever wanted to find was a cure
The adults were never the ones to guide me
I saw nobody beside me
Heard everyone's muffled cries from miles apart
But nobody was ever aware of my screaming heart

Continual

I stand for the right things in the wrong battles

So I'm always the one convicted of treason

Continually in repairs with scaffoldings all year round, I am submerged

Will my gravels drown me, or are my broken parts worthy of being preserved

I'm sorry my breakdowns were an inconvenient view

I was never self-deprecating before I met you

I used to write letters to the deceased and bury it deep

Now, I can say I was naive

I know what I should be thinking, and then I feel the other way

I know what I should be listening to, but I hear different sayings

Being an incandescent, trying not to let my light blind the dull

In a world of mediocrity, I try to fit in

Only to watch myself smile in the photos I appear in

Fixing myself even though I was never broken

I can see my civility has been the token

People see me now, even though the real me is long gone

Mirror Mirror on the wall

The knowledge I crave has been put on a scale
If my respect is based on the score, then what if I fail?
Oh, mirror mirror on the wall, is my pen mightier than all?
I'm squeezing my brain to let it drop on my answer sheet
I've been put in this crowd to get slaughtered like meat
Mirror mirror on the wall, all I do is scrawl

The weight of academia is giving me a cramped limb
What if I drown rather than swim?
Oh mirror, mirror on the wall when death finds me, I want to be alive
I want to be thriving rather than merely surviving
Am I a stain on the system?
Am I too doltish for any words of wisdom?
Mirror Mirror on the wall will I ever belong?

School success is holy
I fail to feel superior after seeing all the people below me
The validation is pushing me off the brim

Maybe I am a muse for the toppers
My dream will never make their way out of the lockers
Oh, mirror mirror on the wall, I've been watching myself trembling and
tumbling

My empire is crumbling

Even though I try to run at my pace, I feel like a waste

I know it is to help me grow

But I can't break free from the burrow

Oh, mirror mirror on the wall, if only you could help me at all!

If I'm honest

If I'm honest, then I hate myself on most days
I am unable to forgive the people
who did me wrong in mysterious ways
I am unable to look at the bright side
The only response from my body
Is to push down my emotions
Before I hurt somebody
I hate and am jealous of most people
But I don't say these words or
they'll consider me evil
I try to talk and socialize
Watching all dreams being commercialized
I've put reminders of all my miseries
But haven't done the same for my victories
If I'm honest,
I am just a kid trying to make it big
But I'm sick of this particular life
Where I've been told what to say
and how to behave
Because of this, I hate myself on most days

Colonnade

I am driving a car with rusted keys
between the colonnade of trees
The road used to be my favorite
Now, I don't remember
how to savor it
The scene only reminds me
of all the people I have lost
during the journey
Which is a lot more than I've met
Feeling too much can be a curse
Especially when you don't know
how to converse
I've become good at being sad
It is happiness that I have banned
Any light of it seems to make me drive away
between the colonnade of trees
with my pair of rusted keys

The desire

There's a desire to be loved and known

And there's a desire to be forgotten and ignored

You'll never see how hard I tried

You'll never know how much I died

I kept showing up as I was drowning in the salt of my tears

With a bag of unanswered prayers

There's a desire to be restrained and silenced

and there's a desire to be vocal and resilient

I want to wipe my past

Erase all the traces on the sand

While someone holds my hand

There's a desire to be looked after

and there's a desire to not have a protector

I let people in to push them away

There's a constant silent rage inside me

and I've never had anyone to guide me

Set myself up for failure and complain

I carry a pain that I can't quite explain

I float on the black canvas painted with stars

I hide my stories because they get impatient when I mention my scars

There's a desire to be rescued

and there's a desire to fight alone

I want them to read my mind to be able to soothe me

All I felt like was an inconvenience to all who knew me

So, I kept showing up for myself
to silence the voice in me that only yells
and become the woman I needed as a girl
and the girl I needed as a woman

I once loved a rebel

Would you bear witness to her madness
when she protests all the time
that makes you want to tarnish your canvas
Would you wait when she goes violent
for she doesn't know what made her mind go silent this time

"I don't want to be the symptom of your disease."
She screams in her sleep
"where justice goes to the one with power,
where people are terrified of their own morals
I don't want to be the by-product of your ignorance
for you can't stand a woman who is vigorous."
Would you cross her barbed wires that might make you bleed
only to let her know how unconditional love feels?

Would you call her brave for standing against everyone
for the sake of those who can't afford to speak
or would you blame her for ruining everything beautiful that comes her
way with her attitude
when choosing to fight her battles, standing over the ground of her
gratitude?

"I have walked the roads they did, but all my idols died young."
the confession slips from her tongue

"I can't go back to where I came from
but this path has become too lonely to walk on
and I have felt too much to succumb
would I ever have anyone to call me 'the one'"

Petition

All the unheard and heard stories
have made my mind wander in the forbidden forest
All the tinkling of the ivories
make my heart race faster than any pair of eyes
The ones I called my hope are the ones
who taught me how to live without it
Stenographer in a room of windbags

Their words are inked on my skin
and there is no room left for another false grin
I only stare at my ceiling, which gleams at night like a sea
I only beg those illuminating stars to hold me
I only yell when nobody can hear my void
I only pray to the god of death, asking
if the signs of love had been destroyed
My body crumbles at a glimpse of hope now
and I sabotage every scope

I only pray to the god of horror, for I am no warrior
My muscles unfold at the thought of another one to hold
With emotional intimacy an alienated concept for them
With consent, a foreign land for them

I only pray to the god of condemn

to let me come down the ladder
and take the best out of waste
but the rungs below me are broken
and I'd rather be alone than around false devotion

Raw

I would jump at the opportunity of being anyone else

Oh, guardian angel, take away my insecurities

in exchange for some maturity

Wash away these acne scars

I fear power, but I want to be with the monarchs

I want to make my own name, but I yearn for old money

Even I wouldn't ask myself on one knee

This world runs away from strong love; they want something less

to keep complaining about something more

Have trust issues, but I'm an open book for false virtues

On seeing my reflection in a crowded room

even I wouldn't dare to ask for a dance with me

Oh, guardian angel, undo me

It's too early for me to be inside my grave

Happiness tends to outrun me each time

Nobody answers my face time

I don't know where I'm heading

Holding the map of this city,

I seem to be walking on a directionless road

I'm too far away to turn around

I'm too lost to ask for help

and it is too dark to see the road ahead

Crying Yellow Tears

I wasn't allowed to gleam about my glories
"Hear all my stories!"
I wasn't allowed affection
"Think of me as perfection!"
I wasn't allowed to cross the wires
"Wash away all my fires!"
They all conspired against me
"You are the key to making me free!"
My secrets were stripped naked
"A humble abode you must make it!"
Was a forlorn figure on the steps of my stairs
"You are to make all the repairs!
Look what happened to me as a kid!
Look what wounds I wasn't to feel!
You are not a doctor, but
undo the stitches and help me heal!"

GRACE

Respect

The concept of 'never giving up' sold to me at a price of my own peace
Podcasts after podcasts
Everyone faded when my tears radiated on a broadcast
Blamed me for not being able to shine
I kept count of the masters whenever my crayons went out of line
The depth of frustration bloated in size
Doing the things I did not like to be able to match your eyes
Lying people told me how to seek truth in life
and I ended up keeping myself on the blade of a knife
Cherry-picking my life to glorify
To seek validation, even if it was for a while
I was not able to save my violet nights
So, I saved myself from these internal fights
We aren't the same; you compared me with others' success
and I, with my own progress
Daily discovery of myself made me feel clean
I came back stronger, like a queen
You were color blind, failed to see how I shined
Broke the chains I was embracing
Proving you my worth isn't something worth chasing
I see my reflection in the right direction
and I will write my own story of the resurrection

Three-Ring Circus

Bouncing from one trampoline to another
Around the clowns, acrobats and jugglers
These "big tops" have been moving around since the 19ᵗʰ century
Nothing seems to be different for a kid like me
All the crowds averted when they saw my lips tremble
The ventriloquist stealth on watching my tears dissemble
I only spoke the language of empirical
and on questioning my masters
I was sent to the asylum
How much weight did you think my weary back could carry?
How much sorrow did you think my heart could bury?
It was the three-ring circus making my mind go crazy
while they all questioned my sanity
I ran from the places who merely saw me as a skin on bones
and willingly exiled myself from all these clones
So go ahead and tell the toddlers about my vampire fangs
but not the story of how they tied my hands
with the ropes that I fabricated
Nobody's tongue slipped when I was to be advocated
So go ahead and keep all your spirits away from my home
for only I had the courage to waltz around their treacherous thrones

Swim

I didn't learn how to swim to watch myself drown

I didn't break down the walls to lose the wars

I didn't learn how to run to collide

I didn't learn the route to let you be my guide

I will run through the fire to rise higher

I learned to be mature to keep the kid alive within me

Who is to free me from the shackles and fight my battles if not me

Broken glass shines the brightest

I'll heal myself every time, even if it hurts in private

Skyfall

The things I have been losing weren't mine to keep
The paths I was once choosing weren't meant for my steps
I have been wandering in places like a forager
Digging every piece of dirt to find a place good enough
Living in a slum within a town full of mansions
You'll never see my worth by putting me on a scale of dearth
Maybe I am stuck in a perpetual skyfall
but I'd rather lose it all than never have tried at all

Pipe Dream

I thought making you proud

would make you come around

Little did I know I was meant to be a wasted curve

I have been walking around you in circles in hopes

you would see yourself treating me like a circus

You might not like who I am, but I do

You made a line, and I was only to walk on the alignment

Had to prove myself when I wasn't done figuring out myself

Kept all my heartbreaks to myself

Kept all the pieces of my shattered faith to myself

Was afraid of what you'd think I am turning out to be

Choking every second of the life you chose for me

You might not like who I am, but I do

I'm walking in a haze, feeling anytime I will accidentally jump off the edge

Slowly but finally, I'm letting go of the heavy hands on my shoulder

Making the best out of the waste I am

One day, I'll say I am happy with how things turned out and mean it

You still might not like who I am, but I do

To the Bullies

You justify your behavior with a sad story pinned on your maps

Rightful narratives of wrongful acts

(It's not my fault)

Sleepless nights to the victims

Ignorance and callousness are your symptoms

(It's not my fault)

Blaming others for your misery so you could sleep gently

I did nothing to let you resent me

(It's not my fault)

I madly dug through the soil to find the roots

Somehow, I'll be able to explain our disputes

(It's not my fault)

It takes so little to be kind

The light can show colors to a blind

(It's not my fault)

My brain is covered in a blue haze

My passive-aggressive behavior has led me to this maze

(It's not my fault)

Unable to articulate it through my words doesn't mean it didn't ache

Devoid people of hope when that's all they can put on stake

(It's not my fault)

Your ruthless behavior has no explanation

I end up screaming, "It's not my fault", at the end of each unshared

conversation

(It's not my fault)
Until then, my ink and quill will shield my attacks
Your remorse will never fill the cracks
(It was never my fault!)

Women

Bold, graceful, surreal and warrior-like are the women in my life
Bold enough to be vulnerable
Graceful enough to pick themselves up
Surreal enough to care for everyone
Warrior-like to fight for themselves
I may not be lucky in eternal love, but I have been lucky in lessons
I may not be lucky in the lottery, but I've been lucky in reshaping my principles
The women around me have taught me to not believe everything and anything that's been told
To make mistakes and learn from them
To educate myself to be able to listen to what others have to say
To have the courage to be vulnerable so that I can offer more love
To how to let humiliation make you stronger and how to let strength make you humble
To provide yourself so you are able to provide for the less fortunate
To unlearn stereotypes so you don't confide people in a box
To love yourself so you are able to heal others
To be your true self to be able to liberate people around you
To be powerful so you know when to be kind
To not let love be an excuse for being stifled
The women around me have taught me the importance of empathy
so that I never stop learning how to be a better person in my misery

Winter is over

We both have demons we can't stand
My alter ego won't let me be with you
You call these excuses; I call them reasons
You took my tolerance for laxity
You came like a blanket during winters
Now it's summer, and you are no good to me
You held my hand and walked me to my doorstep
while I was lost in the radiation fog
I am grateful to you, but now you have become too big to fit into my
house
You pulled me out of the dark only to push me into a graveyard
I was too emotional to have any self-respect
I kept you on a pedestal
Saw your vices disguised as maturity
Now I can see through your bluff, and I can't even stand to see your
shadow
Thought you'd be my forever muse
but you only saw me as a lover's ruse
I don't remember the crash
I only remember the blood
You are a step I had to take to reach my wiser self
but now I can be my own blanket
Am I being hyperbolic or making an understatement
It is a secret I will keep in my casket

Am I stupid or Brave?

From the cradle to the grave
I've been fighting armies stronger than my reason
Am I stupid or brave?

I find the pinholes in all the systems
How do I choose the least misbehaving person?
Am I stupid or brave?

All the times they have stepped on me
Have got their footprints engraved over my skin
Do I waive it off or scrub it and make them pay?
Will that make me stupid or brave?

Shall I fight alone if need be
or smile and nod when they see me
Am I stupid or brave to walk with
the ones who peel my sanity off?

If I don't break the chain
then my next generation will
have to bear the pain
I'll keep my neck on the blade
Even if that makes me stupid or brave

SOCIETAL ABUSE

Moral Combat

My body is considered weak, and yours as strong as a machine
My "no" acting like a bow hitting their egos is obscene
It's not my fault this world sexualized everything about me
Teaching me how to fly, then cutting off my wings to make way for the
kings
I won't take the blame on myself, for you to have an answer
Speaking up doesn't mean victimizing self
Denying the existence of privileges while holding their alcoholic beverages
Every now and then, I hear dirt being thrown on the ones who stand
Every woman I know has been assaulted, but I don't know any suspects
Remember the names of the rape survivor but not of the criminals
Competing in who got it worse, men or women
Forgetting rights for both comes under human rights
"Sexism happens, but the effects of " Reverse sexism" On men are worse."
If you say the same to them, they all defend themselves
yet somehow, everyone's defenseless for you

The Man of the Hour

A shoulder to cry on for everyone
My pain is not to be told to anyone
A can of cheap beer each night
to help me gulp down the silent battles I fight
The savior of each calamity
has nobody to talk to during his tragedy
"A tear is a man's biggest enemy"
This is what I believe has become my identity
I've to put down someone to lift myself up in my tribe
Being callous is the new style; they describe
I am to look smart and healthy
I have to be wise and wealthy
Nobody knows about the mole on my chest
Each day I'm trying to give my best
Numerous roles I'm supposed to play with a smile on my face
Broad shoulders and pumped biceps
I'm losing myself on each step

The Filthy One

I know who has been inside my temple
but I didn't choose it to be my sacred place
Aggressively trespassing
Why am I the one who has lost grace?
His intoxicated soul still lingers around my air
Evil eyes everywhere, ogling on everything I wear
I believe it's not my fault, but I'm told otherwise
Pity and sympathy is all I get now
Trying to pack these haunting memories forever
but then I see the frown in the brow
Nobody sees me for who I am anymore
I am defined as a victim or a survivor
My name is all over the news while his face is covered to not let his
identity run lose
The rage is expected to wash away
The retribution is given based on my reaction
despite the action causing me grave dismay
There lies dirt in the eyes of the system
The abused is the one smeared
The sinewy is to be feared
Everyone expects me to be in a burial shroud or to conceal myself from
the crowd
These guilty eyes are screeching at my smile
In this insurmountable pain, I choose to hold on to myself tight

Double Lies

A business deal is how I look at it

Bucks to afford two cups

*Those who know me take a few steps back and think of me as a
contagious disease*

Nobody questions my clients, going ahead and doing what they please

The double standards of being a bawd

The minds of the system are flawed

Money, despite being black, lurks around in broad daylight

Everybody sees the gender during the verdict they write

The prejudices are ingrained as reality

Turns a blind eye to their own brutality

Stain the faces of other women with acid for not being accepted

Nodding to whatever is being told

For them, using their own brain is not gold

These paradoxes where everyone is pummeling each other

Where fists talk before the mouths can utter

I hold no responsibility to change their minds

because the sinners stand on both sides

Irony

Compliments I have to take nicely when they are trying to make a move
on me slyly
If I say it with a smile, then they ask me again
If I say it firmly, then they call me a prude
Comparing myself with other women makes me feel special
I am always blamed for not being careful
Have to choose between being sentimental and being a rebel
Not sending me out after dark for even the men bark
Expected me to be docile and tamed
or I will be too opinionated
Expected me to speak softly
or I will be loud and obnoxious
Expected to smile and nod politely
Even when I have nothing to smile about
Expected me to dream big
and then cease after my wedding
Expected to want to have a family
and then make me feel guilty for not feeling motherly
Expected me to love my children
and the husband to be distant
Daily self-talks to break this internalized misogyny from my head
Daily self-questioning to move past these double standards
to become an adult, I needed to be a kid
Will be an outcast than to bore such a past

Vie

Sudden tears rolling down crimson cheeks

in a snap, they roll away

Books making her walk through thousand minds

Escape reality to loosen up the familiarity

Pleasure is what she reads for

Gets paranoid if you put her on a scale

"What if I underscore?"

Oar is what she is desperately searching for

Running away from this town before her mind is forced to vie

She doesn't want to comply

Her breathing passion has turned inanimate

You learn by failing, yet everyone wants you to master everything

A Hopeful gleam in her parents' eyes sends a chill up and down her
spine

Trying her best to take the highest dive before the wolves eat her alive

Drinking but not assimilating the answers to every question

Everything seems like a scribble

She slickly has been put inside this riddle

Cheap Games

The camera clicks, and all they do is lie
We can't do anything but try
These people are busy filling their own pockets
while our future is being sold in black markets
They'd paint all our skies gray
Leaving us in dismay
They can't take away our morals
They can't take away our empathy
They can't take away our respect
I know we are too tired to carry on
but it's only a matter of time
for us to be standing against these crimes

Patriarchy

I can only remember but not react

I can only say what you please

I can only stand for what you believe

I have to answer every question asked

I have to let my waist be a resting place

I have to smile for not making a scene

I have to be sweet to be liked

I have to question my sense of judgment

when an unwanted hand is on my garment

I have to cook in sickness or in health

and you can only do it on the weekends

I have to fit into a corset to be a treat to your eyes

I have to apologize for not asking for masculine help

I have to be ok with you leering because of my damp hair

I have to wear short dresses to be looked at but still not be taken seriously

I have to let go of the cerebral equality

I have to remove every hair on my skin to be played like a violin

I tried, but I can't oversee

I tried, but I can't be the bigger person

You feed me my favorite meals to keep me happy

You let go of my one hand and chained the rest of me

I react on emotions, and somehow, you are a strategic

and here I see men pouring acid on simply being rejected

You constantly reminded me of every step you took toward me

as if I am supposed to be grateful
You put me in a cage and threw away the keys
I radiated my energy like the sun to melt these
I am not made of paper mache or plastic wood
that you'd make me dance around in whatever way you could
I have my own mind and free will
I have my own voice and quill
and I will not surrender until
I get all of us at the top of the hill

You are WHAT YOU DID

You were convicted but never got time
You were the face of the crime
but didn't pay a dime
You hid your face in the darkness during the felony
ingraining a blip inside my memory

All the speakers kept my past frozen behind a glass
and my character behind bars
My identity revolves around one incident
and spirit revolving around the haunted house

The protector of the realm was a part of such a calamity
The protector of the realm lured his hands into places
making it a tragedy

"Not all men" acting as the devil's advocate
My body always making me feel inadequate
If home is supposed to be heaven
then send me straight to hell

I took the abuse
while you used my hands to seduce
Tell me, how many came before me?
Tell me, how many came after me?

I might accept your insanity as the reason behind my tragedy
but I will never be able to teach the abused kid the good side of trust
when your mind couldn't go beyond lust

If home is supposed to be heaven
then send me straight to hell

GRIEF

After My Demise

Will your smile fade away once you hear my name
Will you walk away from the places where we made our memories at
Will you look away when you see my face in the photos you clicked, not
knowing forever meant ephemeral
Will you try to erase my existence to be able to breathe without choking
Would you have my photo on the wall with a beautiful garland you
picked after the rainfall
Would you hate the disease that spread like lightning inside me
Will you watch me slipping away from you in your dreams
How long will it take you to remember how to have a heartbeat
When will you untie your tongue to tell my mischief tale
and when you do so, will you always have salt in your eyes
Which day would be worse, my birthday or the last time I was able to
see the colors of this world?

Losing People

*My affection makes me wonder of the day their soul will turn into a
ghost*
Trying to prepare me for the worst
I'm afraid of all the unexpressed love that will torment me the most
but I can't tell them how they make me feel
My words will eventually ruin the beautiful things
My dreams weave the thought of losing them
Making me grieve before the time

Won't Tell Anyone

I wouldn't whisper in the dark about the agony that resides within me
The torment of not being able to love my lover
You were a rose that made me bleed from the thorns
You had a lot to offer me, but you always took it away in a snap
You let me dream of places you weren't worthy of being in
You let me wonder about the brightness while you were incapable of
shining from within
You threw nickels and let me wonder about the diamonds
Your deceitful words made me deaf to the sirens
Now your carcass lies seven feet under the soil I stand on
Do I love you as a good person, or move on?
Do I write a eulogy or talk about reality?
You said you loved me, but it sounded like
you were reading lines out loud for a nominee
Losing somebody can be a win-win
but we aren't supposed to think I'll of the dead
This guilt assembled by the anger is layered in each thread
Do I think of you as benevolent even though now it's all irrelevant?
One shouldn't think ill of the dead
but I can't erase the merciless things you said

Mother Without a Child

How do you grieve over someone who you never got to love
How do you cry over a loss you never experienced
The blood lumps from my vagina is the closest I got to you
This pain is too big to whisper about
This lovelorn is too unbearable to even think about
You don't have a face in my memory, but I'd burn the city
if that's what it takes to hold you for a microsecond
Bad things are just blessings in disguise;
My faith is timeless but what blessing makes a mother childless?

Final Goodbye

I'll miss you till I die
but I need to let you go
because sometimes
feeling safe
is more important
than feeling loved

Do You Miss Him?

How do I miss someone who only reminded me of the worst parts of me?

ASSEMBLED HOPE

Rope Of Hope

When all the sunlight fades in the darkness of the night
When you don't have warm clothes to shield yourself from the cold whips
of the winter
Hold on to the rope of hope
When the polluted sky covers the stars
When all you can see are old wounds becoming new scars
When you can't remember what better felt like
Hold on to the rope of hope
When other's love is not reaching your doorstep
When you don't know whether to take a half-step, whole step, overstep
or side-step
When your pain is ineffable
When you are running on empty, and nothing is accessible
Hold onto the rope of hope
When you are the tired one
When you can't turn to anyone
Easier said than done
but hold onto the rope of hope
When you don't know what went wrong
When you don't know if this battle will be lifelong
Hold onto the rope of hope
because there's always a twist at the end of every trope

By Me

The anxious tears made me smile

The dullness made me shine

That foggy brain cleared my sky

The shivering surface taught me how to ground myself

The fear ended up calming my flight

The darkness guided me to the light

The fall taught me how to fly

I had to shrink to grow

Had to drown to dive

Had to choke to breathe

Had to be buried to bloom

It was all created by me for the better me

When I Find the One

Will I be able to tell you about my demons

or will I be tormented by my past?

Will our love heal my half-mended heart

or will the blood from my shattered pieces stain your art?

Will I be able to cry without being judged

or will my emotions have to adjust?

Will I be able to offer you more than you deserve

or will dry love run in every nerve?

Will I be able to tell you my side of the story

or will you, too, never trust my glory?

Will I be able to trust more freely

or will my insecurities crawl in discreetly?

Will I be able to live in the moment

or will fear of losing you lead me to encroachment?

The Book On Your Shelf

These words were written by me

These words that I have heard, read, and processed

These words that have been rephrased

Are now sitting on somebody's shelf

No one word, No one line, No one dialogue can help you walk the mile

Yet I'm scouring this piece of my paper

To help someone make a brighter future

To be able to wash away the pain from your past

Trying to fit the right words in each line

to pull you out of this plight

I'm trying to write the words I wanted to hear,

when the pain got too much to bear

So many pages above, these words

So many pages below these words

Sometimes, in the middle of nowhere, you find yourself

like you found these words lying here, waiting to be seen, all by yourself

Was I of any help, or are my words just sitting on your shelf?

Music

Cluster of words
synchronizing my feet on the beat
Never paying lyrics any heed
Now, they define my void soul
Helped me make words from the alphabet
Voices of different kinds
making me sound sane in my mind
An old song plays on the radio, and I start
reminiscing the moments associated
The verse has made my layers exfoliated
Every song is an epiphany
Giving me solace and making me free
I'll never be lost as long as I have this with me

Definition

I'm not defined by the things I fear
Not defined by the past that led me here
Not by the souls who walked away from me
The ones I tried to love faithfully
I've fallen in love and out of it
Have tried multiple lives, and even more, I've quit
Not by the corporate position I hold
Not by the things I was told
Not by the way you endear me based on the success that I never wanted
within me

The sound of laughing innocently
The wind blows on my face gently
The beat that makes me tap my feet
The golden hour coloring the world around me
The visions that astound me
The acoustic version of nature
The words I pour on paper
The dew on the grass touching my bare skin
The emotions that reside within
The bath in the sun at noon
The birds dancing around a cloudy sky
I'm defined by all the things that give me a happy cry

Loneliness

The isolation that arises from assembling your shattered pieces with grace
where everyone thinks you're brave
The lingering loneliness between trying to figure out who you are while
grieving the loss of the old you
A phase where you are recovering from all the battle wounds
A new person can sweep you off your feet again, but you are peculiarly
particular this time
of trying not to encourage another crime
Not wanting to choose from the poor options you have
Avoiding another whiplash
Constantly pushing yourself to pull yourself together
More people won't help you get better
Living with yourself is the biggest challenge
It's all in creating a balance
You've to be your own critic and your own cheerleader
but honey, life will get sweeter

Not a Religious Person

I am not a religious person, but sometimes the weight on my shoulders gets heavy
I want to believe that God let me borrow his when life got tricky
Makes me believe there's an angel in hell and a Satan in heaven
Not seeking every story as a lesson
Some moments are only there for succession
I am not a religious person, but I love how festivals make us all come together
giving us an excuse to appreciate each other
I am not a religious person, but I want to believe in higher energy
That there's a path I'm being made to walk on to get in touch with my identity

Judge Yourself

It's not easy to not judge yourself for not wanting to run a phantom race
where everyone is expecting you to act in a certain way
to not want the same things as others
for not wanting a big fancy house with only a handful of people living
in
for not wanting to own the most expensive brands
for prioritizing your time over money
for not wanting to have any regrets on your deathbed
for wanting to do things that make you happy and not leave others
satisfied
for not wanting to be on a scale for social points
for dressing for comfort and not to impress
for not having too many friends
It's not easy to rest without thinking you've given up
It's not easy to walk through life when everyone is asking you to run

Black Hole

I have been in and out before
within the darkness that resides in my soul
like I am its favorite guest
Doesn't seem to let go and rest
Its force is too strong, like a black hole
Sucks me in every time I see a glimmer of hope
With all my strength, I rip the invisible strings
and hope to be saved by the spring
It's an unpicked game
and all the plays are the same
The only thing that keeps me going
The only thing I cling onto
is the hope to be saved by the spring

Nostalgia

Nostalgia has been a constant reminder of the paradox I live in

It is an excruciating feeling of longing

It is a serene feeling of belonging

I keep colluding to run from the companions of it

The sorrows that come with

I hold my breath while walking the streets,

the ones who gave me daily treats

A hug from a tempest

Familiar with this feeling because my dad is a lieutenant

Frightened of making new memories

feel like I will end up on the same streets

but I can't seem to dust off the inclusion I feel and how it makes me

feel complete

The fact that I am making memories is a sole reminder of my breathing

Who Am I?

I am the pearl at the depth of the sea
and I am the wave running to the shores
I am the master of my ship
and I am the wood of my boat
I am the pain and the agony
I am the bliss and the epiphany
I am everything, and I am nothing
I am all the planets in the solar system and
I am the ones that go undiscovered
I am the starving child and the pretzeled mind
I am the wisdom, and I am the foolishness
I am everything, and I am nothing

Moving On

Watching everyone living their lives from the rearview
Everything is gray or blue
and my bedsheets smell of salt from all the crying I've done the past year
or two
One
Two
Three
I want the confidence I had when I was fifteen
Everyone deciding what's best for me
Caging me in and asking me to stretch my wings
Tying up my legs and asking me to run
Comparing myself with other kids while not letting me discover myself
One
Two
Three
I see our clocks are set in different time zones
and none is ahead or behind
I was caught up in a high tide
Now I see the rules of the game,
You have to play at your own pace without any shame
One
Two
Three
It's not about not being good enough

It's about that thing not being enough for

you to be good at

Watch the Sky Once in a While

Wait up kid

You've been running too fast

for your time

It has all been planned out for you

Look up and enjoy the view

I know you have plans

but you've only got two hands

Wait up kid

Take one step at a time or

you're bound to burn out

You can't outrun time

The reward might be worth a dime

but it's the process that's sublime

Wait up kid

The voices that are getting louder and louder by the day

Will fade away with each step of the way

Look up and watch the birds around the clouds

Looking like black pepper

because you won't have this view forever

'Til Death Do Us Part

I just hope love finds you in this lifetime
and when it does, you allow yourself to let it in
even if it has no intention of staying

My Torn Journal

Decluttering my old desk
I found a massive wreck
of all the things I once thought were important
have now left my life without a warrant

I found a half-torn journal
The binding was off and
the pages lay like a blanket
over a bracelet my friend gave me
while promising to stay in touch forever
Wilted Daffodils, my ex, gifted me
while vowing to love me forever
The pages were looking back at me
surrounded by other things I can't recall

Reading the things I had rambled upon these pages
made me feel uneasy
Reminiscing about winning all the battles
I didn't want to fight
All the tears that stitched my wounds
All the panic attacks that I turned into my muse
and all the voiceless screams I turned into my favorite symphony

Lately, I could only see the road that lay ahead
Now, these torn pages act as a mirror of my past
A mirror that helps me see all that I surpassed

I dashed out of my room into the balcony
for I deserve a break, a pat on the back
even if there lies a long road ahead of me
I still can feel proud without feeling guilty

If I Am Not Here Tomorrow

Scatter it all over the place
Scatter, the unexpressed love all over the people
You didn't have a say in how I was to be taken away, and neither did I
When my face fades away from your dreams
When you start to forget the scent I used to wear
When you can't remember what my voice sounded like
When you can't recall my favorite cuisine
Don't be afraid; let it all fade away

Love exists in the memories, in the chest,
in every fraction of the body, and it only truly dies with the soul
but I'll die in heaven watching you feeling alone
To watch you give yourself a hard time every time you had a long laugh
Smile, even if it's only for a while
I've been here before when I was breathing and gasping
when I was shivering and couldn't comprehend
I've been here before when the evil resided in my head

but this time, I'm not scared
Let your tears fall when the grief intensifies
Feel my love when you bathe in the sun
Feel my laugh when you hear the leaves rustle
I'll be cheering you on like the branches sway

Feel my kiss when the waves wash your feet
Be assured, I'm at peace

Canvas

I painted the canvas with vibrant colors

for it to catch your eyes

I splashed white as a way of going back in time

I painted the canvas using a vintage pastel palette

I splashed white, for I have no talent

I don't want this journey to end, but I am too scared to start

What side do I pick:

Losing the battle against perfectionism at the cost of my humility

or winning the battle against perfectionism at the cost of my sanity?

Am I ever going to escape reality?

I splashed white one last time

to start something worth a nickel or a dime

Use this blank canva to write your perfectly imperfect poem :)

www.ingramcontent.com/pod-product-compliance
Lightning Source LLC
Chambersburg PA
CBHW021538150726
47990CB00006B/2294